100% UNOFFICIAL

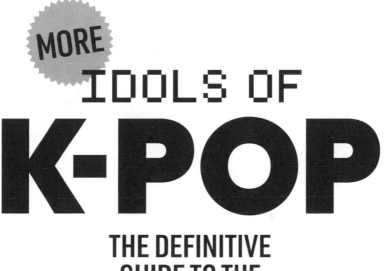

MORE

IDOLS OF
K-POP

THE DEFINITIVE
GUIDE TO THE
HOTTEST BANDS

Natasha Mulenga

First published in Great Britain 2022 by Dean,
part of Farshore
An imprint of HarperCollins*Publishers*
1 London Bridge Street, London SE1 9GF
www.farshore.co.uk

HarperCollins*Publishers*
1st Floor, Watermarque Building, Ringsend Road
Dublin 4, Ireland

Written by Natasha Mulenga
Designed by Ian Pollard

This book is an original creation by Farshore © 2022 HarperCollinsPublishers Limited

ISBN 978 0 7555 0229 5
Printed in Italy
001

100% UNOFFICIAL

MORE

IDOLS OF

K-POP

THE DEFINITIVE
GUIDE TO THE
HOTTEST BANDS

Natasha Mulenga

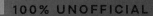

12 BTS

20 MAMAMOO

CONTENTS

34 BLACKPINK

16 ERIC NAM

THE HISTORY OF
K-POP

Welcome to the crazy world of K-Pop. Let us take you on a journey through the history of South Korean music.

THE CULTURAL EXCHANGE

The rise of western-influenced music in Korea can be traced back as far as 1885, when a missionary (that's someone who travels abroad to share their religious beliefs) named Henry Appenzeller began to teach western folk songs to schoolchildren, replacing the original English lyrics with Korean ones. These new-sounding songs were known as *changga* and often denounced Korea's oppressors (otherwise known as throwing shade, peeps).

The songs were quickly banned by the Japanese when they ruled over Korea in the first half of the twentieth century. Then, after Korea gained its independence from Japan, the peninsula was partitioned into North and South, causing the Korean war, with American popular music filtering into Korea via the U.S. troops. Over time, western culture gradually became more accepted, and pop music derived from the old *changga* songs became known as *Trot. Trot* music started to sound more American and it was at this time that the first Korean pop stars, The Kim Sisters, rose to popularity.

Seo Taiji and Boys performing *I Know* on MBC's music show in 1992.

Paving the way ...

NEW SOUNDS

The Korean music scene was dominated by *Trot* until the group Seo Taiji and Boys came onto the scene. They are considered the founders of modern K-Pop. Their first televised performance on MBC in 1992 was a defining moment. Their song 난 알아요 (*I Know*) was an upbeat mix of rap and ballad, and instantly resonated with Korean youth. They were ready for a new style of dance music fused with hip-hop, borrowing ideas from African-American culture. Despite getting the lowest score of the night, the song went on to top the charts and remained there for 17 weeks.

K-PIONEERS

Seo Taiji and Boys used their new fame to speak for their young fans and the issues they faced. Their track *Classroom Idea* heavily criticised the South Korean school system and the pressure young students were facing, while gangster-rap *Come Back Home*, explored Taiji's experience of running away from home. Though they retired in 1996, their impact – fighting censorship, challenging fashion norms – laid foundations for the entire industry and set a blueprint for what record labels looked for in the next teen sensation. Phew, job done, Boys!

Sunglasses, hats and gloves ... it was a look!

THE VETERANS

Allow us to introduce ... the idols of K-Pop who built a multi-billion dollar industry (that's a lot of downloads!)

BoA

BoA is widely known as the Queen of K-Pop. The singer-songwriter was only 14 when she debuted under SM Entertainment in 2000. At 16, she became the first Korean artist to achieve success in Japan and she was also the first K-Pop artist to attempt a breakthrough in the U.S. This over-achieving idol has released 20 albums, writes, produces and acts!

WONDER GIRLS

The quintet from JYP Entertainment. *Nobody* was the first Korean song to appear on Billboard's Hot 100 and contributed to the rise of iconic Hallyu (Korean wave) stars that includes groups 2NE1, Girls' Generation and KARA.

Big Bang literally have the world in their hands ...

BIG BANG

Big Bang formed in 2006 under YG Entertainment. The group sold 140 million records over the course of their career, and in 2015 the *Hollywood Reporter* called them "The Biggest Boyband In The World". Big Bang's G-Dragon has more registered song credits than any other creator in K-Pop leading to his nickname 'The King of K-Pop.'

The winners of the generation game.

GIRLS' GENERATION

SNSD (which is a short form of the group's Korean name, So Nyeo Shi Dae) became the first Asian girl group to achieve five music videos (M/Vs) with over 100 million views on YouTube with *Gee*, *I Got a Boy*, *The Boys*, *Mr. Taxi*, and *Oh!*. Having an international presence was practically unheard for K-Pop stars until Girls' Generation came along.

2NE1

It would be criminal (don't arrest us!) to not include 2NE1. Known for their edgy style and charisma, they were a breath of fresh air from the more clean-cut girl groups at the time. They sold a whopping 66.5 million records!

PSY

Who can forget the impact that *Gangnam Style* had on the world? PSY's unforgettable song is the most viewed YouTube video ever (currently sitting at 3.8 billion views). The iconic track reached number 2 on the Billboard Hot 100 in 2012, which was monumental for K-Pop. But don't let this playful song fool you, PSY is a well-respected artist in South Korea, who sells out stadiums and arenas. Jessi, Hyuna, Dawn, Crush and Heize are all signed to his label P-Nation.

THE K-POP
MACHINE

Explore the extraordinary industry working behind the scenes of K-Pop, and keeping everything on track.

THE TRAINEE SYSTEM

Aspiring idols attend auditions or are scouted by entertainment companies. Idols then go through training (basically K-Pop school), where they learn how to sing, dance, write music and learn different languages such as Japanese and English. By the time a singer or group debuts their music, they are ready to take on the world! The trainee process can take months or years depending on the individual. Most trainees are recruited when they

ITZY making their majestic moves. Iconic.

are teenagers but not every trainee ends up making music. It really is survival of the fittest.

COMEBACKS

K-Pop artists put music out at a faster rate than most Western artists. A 'comeback' (the release of new music) can happen once or twice a year: more music and content certainly means happier fans! Comebacks will be heavily promoted: singers will tease fans with concept photos and previews for their upcoming M/V; and the album and lead single will drop simultaneously.

New ambassadors for Korean culture (and cool!): LOONA.

Acts will perform songs from the new album on all the popular music shows (such as *M Countdown* and *Inkigayo*); artists will upload dance practices of their new songs and release the behind the scenes footage of the M/V; and will provide commentary on the album-making process. All of these events are part of the very busy comeback season and all act to promote the new album to their adoring fanbase.

Got7 got our attention with their 'Lullaby' comeback.

EVERYONE GETS A CHANCE TO SHINE

When a member of your fave group decides to go solo it often spells the beginning of the end for the band. Just look at what happened to One Direction after Zayn jumped ship. Well, that's not the case in K-Pop. Under their contracts, every member of a group can release solo songs, mixtapes and albums. Sometimes where there is a large group, members will form a sub-unit and release an album. Super Junior's Donghae and Eunhyuk formed D&E, Super Junior's fifth sub-unit!

Fun in the jungle.

THE M/V

K-Pop fans go crazy over music videos. M/Vs will have themes and stories that will develop into an entire universe throughout the course of an artist's music-making career. BTS fans often create fan-theory videos dissecting details of M/Vs to try and understand what is going on inside the BTS universe. These fact-detecting fans put Sherlock Holmes to shame!

"High five! Up above, down below, too slow." Oh, D&E!

방탄소년단
BTS

When you think of K-Pop, you think of BTS.
You have to, it's the law.

BACKGROUND

BTS first entered the K-Pop scene in 2013 through Big Hit Entertainment. At first they were a hip-hop group, consisting of RM, Suga and J-Hope, but they soon became a regular group. They debuted their song *No More Dream* in 2013. Despite their mega-fame now, it took BTS a while to build up popularity in their home country. Ranking on competitive music shows such as *Music Bank, M Countdown* or *Inkigayo* (a bit like Top of the Pops) is very important to K-Pop groups. Most acts from the three major music agencies achieve a music show win within their first year of debut. However it took BTS two years, only getting their first win in 2015 with their song *I Need U*. They didn't get a lot of recognition from the music industry because they were from a small music company that didn't have a lot money. BTS may have been slow to build success but with a lot of hard work and dedication from the boys, once the ball got rolling there was no stopping them. Theirs is a true underdog story.

> Nothing but Savage Love for the Dynamite looks BTS are serving.

BTS: Breaking through (and breaking hearts) at the Billboard Awards.

ACHIEVEMENTS

● BTS were the first Korean group to perform at the American Music Awards in 2017 and the Billboard Awards in 2018.

● In 2019 BTS sold out Wembley Stadium in 90 minutes and the tour grossed $196.4 million worldwide.

● With a rendition of *Seoul Town Road*, BTS made history as the first Korean artists to perform on the Grammy's stage (in its 60+ years of existence).

● In September 2020, BTS were invited to address the United Nations General Assembly to raise awareness of the issues future generations are facing due to COVID-19.

● Not only are BTS the first Koreans to get a No. 1 on the Billboard Hot 100 but they took three No. 1s in the space of three months. That's unthinkable! *Dynamite*, *Savage Love* (which featured Jason Derulo and Jawsh 685) and *Life Goes On* topped the chart in late 2020.

● *Butter* is the longest-running No. 1 debut by a group in Hot 100 history, sitting at the top of the singles charts for seven consecutive weeks.

● BTS are so successful that 1 in 13 people who visit South Korea go just because of BTS!

FANDOM

● BTS's fans are called ARMY, short for Adorable Representatives M.C. for Youth. Don't let the cute name fool you, their fans are a force to be reckoned with.

BTS

SUGA
슈가

Min Yoongi used to be an underground rapper and joined Big Hit to be a producer. He's an excellent cook and song writer. He's incredibly sweet except when his fierce rap alter ego Agust D takes over on the microphone!
● **Sweet as Suga.**

V
뷔

Kim Taehyung is super friendly. He's into fashion and photography, and has a sultry baritone voice.
● **All hail the Gucci King!**

JIN
진

Kim Seokjin is the oldest, but that doesn't stop him being known as "World Wide Handsome".
● **Official Visual.**

JUNGKOOK
정국

Jeon Jungkook is the youngest. He's nicknamed the Golden Maknae (maknae means youngest) because he's so multi-talented! He even directed BTS's latest M/V for *Life Goes On*.
● **Golden Maknae always shines!**

RM
김남준

Kim Namjoon is otherwise known as RM (Rap Monster) and is the leader of BTS. He was an underground rapper. He learned English watching *Friends*. He has an IQ of 148 (genius-brainbox alert!).

 How you doin'?

JIMIN
지민

Park Jimin is known for being very funny and he is also a perfectionist. Jimin studied contemporary dance before he became a K-Pop trainee.

● **Can we have this dance, Jimin?**

J-HOPE
제이홉

Jung Hoseok is the dance leader of BTS. He has lots of energy and a smile that can light up any room. Check out his solo mixtape release *Hope World*.

● **Who needs a lightbulb? We have J-Hope!**

SOLO STARS

Meet the solo stars shining just for you!

Some idols have so much star power that a group can't contain them. These solo artists want the spotlight all to themselves, and they certainly earn it: making mind-blowing music that ranges from pop to R&B and hip-hop. Meet the solo superstars shining all on their own.

JESSI

Jessi is a Korean American who went to South Korea looking for success. She's known for being a no-nonsense girl who says whatever's on her mind.

HYUNA

Hyuna is a singer who is not afraid to push boundaries. Hyuna started out in girl bands Wonder Girls and 4Minute before going solo and signing with PSY's label. She's a self-styled performance-oriented artist, who focusses as much on her image as her music. Her M/Vs have broken viewing records and her latest drop: *I'm Not Cool* is sure to send her stratospheric!

ERIC NAM

Born and raised in the U.S., Eric Nam is a singer and a tv host. He's interviewed almost all the actors from the Marvel franchise, Will Smith and many more. Eric has his own podcast on DIVE Studios. Plus, his song *Congratulations* is super awesome.

Suran is branching out.

SURAN

Suran is an amazing singer who has the perfect voice for K-Drama soundtracks. Suga from BTS produced her song *Wine*, which won her a host of awards. One to watch!

HYOLYN

Hyolyn was originally part of the group Sistar. Now she has her own label and has released amazing songs like *Dally* and *Say My Name*. Her live vocals are sensational!

JAY PARK

We couldn't talk about solo artists without mentioning Jay Park. He has been a huge pioneer in K-Hip-hop. He runs his own label and is also signed to Jay-Z's label Roc Nation.

DEAN

Dean is considered the King of K-R&B. His voice is so soulful! He's fluent in English and was the first Korean artist to appear on the acclaimed YouTube music show *Colors*.

HEIZE

Heize is one of the most popular solo artists in South Korea. She has such a cool vibe and her songs *And July* featuring Dean and *We Don't Talk Together* are fire!

MOMENTS
THAT ROCKED K-POP

Ground-breaking events that transformed the world of K-Pop!

M/V *Candy*.

H.O.T. SELL 1 MILLION ALBUMS, 1996

The original idols H.O.T. were among the first K-Pop stars to achieve a million-selling album with debut *We Hate All Kinds of Violence*. Filled with energetic and uplifting tracks, including their hit single, *Candy*, the album bagged them Best New Artist at the 1996 Golden Disk Awards.

TVXQ SUE SM, 2009

TVXQ members Jaejoong, Yoochun, and Junsu played a vital role in reducing the length of Korean music contracts. They took SM Entertainment to court in 2009, stating that the agency's 13-year-contract was too long, that they were not in charge of their schedules and that they received almost none of the profits from their success. Following their historic win in court, K-Pop contracts were limited to just 7 years.

M/V *Hug*.

BLACKPINK AT COACHELLA, 2019

BLACKPINK will go down in history as the first Korean girl group to perform at the iconic Californian festival. In their Netflix doc., *Light Up The Sky*, the girls say this was the moment they knew they had made it BIG.

BLACKPINK slaying at *Coachella*.

MTV VMAS CREATE K-POP AWARD, 2019

The world-dominating power of K-Pop cannot be ignored, like, who'd want to!? We know idols regularly get millions of views on YouTube, and sell out arenas across the world. So it kinda makes sense that one of the biggest award shows in music should recognise the work of K-Pop artists. While this is definitely a step in the right direction it would be good to see idols nominated in ALL categories!

BTS representing K-Pop - worldwide!

BTS HIT THE NO. 1 SPOT ON BILLBOARD HOT 100, 2020

BTS broke through a huge barrier for K-Pop when they flew to the top of the U.S. Billboard Hot 100 for not just one but three songs: *Dynamite*, *Savage Love Remix* and *Life Goes On*! What makes their achievement even more special is *Life Goes On* was the first ever non-English language song in the history of Billboard to go straight into the charts at No. 1! The loyal FAN ARMY really does have all the power. BTS is an inspiration!

BTS ARE GRAMMY NOMINEES, 2021

The Grammys are super serious about their music, to win one of their gongs is one of the highest honours a musician can ever receive, like, ever! The internet nearly imploded when it was announced that BTS were the first South Korean artists in history to be nominated for a Pop Award. RM was so excited he threw his phone across the room!

마마무

MAMAMOO

Mamamoo are jazz, retro-pop, and R&B sounds, wrapped in a sophisticated, sensual quartet power package.

BACKGROUND

Mamamoo are now known as some of the best vocalists in the industry, but they had a rocky start. They debuted back in 2014 under a small company called RBW Entertainment. There were originally five members but the last girl dropped out just before their debut EP, *HELLO*, was released alongside lead single *Mr Ambiguous*.

Mamamoo were the first group to debut under RBW and they didn't make much money to begin with, so they were told that they wouldn't make it. In fact, when they were trainees, Solar, Moonbyul and Hwasa all shared a rooftop flat that had cockroaches. Yikes!

Their CEO had also told them that they would have to be exceptional at live performances and singing since they did not fit traditional beauty standards of K-Pop stars. Rude! Cue the hard work. Mamamoo surprised and impressed the industry with their jazz/R&B sound, strong vocals and the fact that they write, produce and compose their own music.

Mamamoo, Mamamazing!

The vocal queens of K-Pop are ready to entertain you.

Idol intensity.

ACHIEVEMENTS

● They won the Rookie of the Year award in 2015 and got their first music show win two years after they debuted. Get it girls!

● Mamamoo got their big break on the show *Immortal Song* where they were recognised and praised for their vocal talents. Not only did they win (which is very rare for a group) but they are the only group to win an amazing three times!

● The quartet have won several awards including Best Vocal Artist at the Mnet Asian Music Awards in 2018 & 2019, Best Group in 2019 at the Golden Disk Awards and Hwasa won Best Solo Artist at the same award show.

● Their 2019 single *Hip* reached No. 1 on Billboard's World Digital Song Sale charts, which is impressive. Mamamoo are unstoppable!

SOLO PROJECTS

Each member has released their own solo songs and mini albums.

● **Hwasa** released *TWIT* in 2019 where she dressed up in plastic in tribute to JYP himself (the former CEO of the big three company JYP). He must have liked it because he joined her on stage in his signature plastic look.

● **Moonbyul** has a song called *Selfish* feat. Seulgi from Red Velvet, which serves serious vibes. She also released her solo mini album in 2020 with the lead single *Eclipse*.

● **Solar** released a single called *Spit It Out* in April 2020. She even got a music show win for it.

● **Wheein** has a solo song called *Easy* feat. Sik-K. The video is so fun and Hwasa even makes a cameo. Wheein also recorded a song called *Shine On You*.

Heart arms, too cute!

MAMAMOO

MOONBYUL
문별이

Moon Byul Yi is one of the best female rappers in K-Pop and has an amazing singing voice too. Moon and Solar like to resolve their disagreements by sending pictures of cute puppies as a way of apologising to each other.
● **Moon shines on stage!**

SOLAR
솔라

Kim Yong Sun is the leader of the group and became a K-Pop trainee at 22, which is older than average. She can play piano and is the third-gen female idol with the most song credits. She has her own YouTube channel and is obsessed with BTS's song *Blood Sweat & Tears*.
● **No one can eclipse our Solar!**

WHEEIN
정휘인

Jung Whee In is a creative in every sense of the word. She can play the piano and drums and loves drawing and painting. She and Hwasa have been BFFs since middle school and used to audition together.

 Talented Wheein draws us in.

HWASA
화사

Ahn Hye-jin is the maknae of the group, and is known for her fearless fashion moments. Hwasa is a true icon of body positivity for her fans. Hwasa has a confident stage presence backed up by her on point vocals and talents in both writing and composing.

 Hwasa dresses to impress.

IDOLS WITH THE
MOVES

These idols effortlessly throw sick moves, flexing on stage and in some insanely choreographed M/Vs.

Taemin slays in M/V *Want*.

TAEMIN
(SHINEE)

In 2006, Taemin won first place on *Hit the Stage*. His M/Vs of *Want*, *Move* and *Criminal* are mind-blowing. He's pioneered an androgynous image that is reflected in his choreography. He makes his moves on a dance-planet all of his own. Out of this world!

LiliFilm #3 is a vibe.

LISA (BLACKPINK)

Lisa definitely deserves her place as No. 1 K-Pop dance idol. Her high-key dance vid *Lilifilm #3* broke the internet with celebs (including Dolly Parton!) superimposing Lisa's legs onto their own images creating hilarious memes.

MOMO (TWICE)

There is a reason Momo is called a 'Dancing Machine'. She practises for hours on end to keep in peak physical condition and perfect her routines. In her spare time, she likes to teach herself choreography for fun, like G-Friend's *Rough* and Red Velvet's *Dumb Dumb*. Give us Momo-more.

Seulgi flexing some moves in M/V *Uncover*.

SEULGI (RED VELVET)

Not only has Seulgi got the props in the vocals department, she also kills it on the dancefloor. She is one of the best dancers at SM Entertainment and has collabed on performances with Taemin (SHINee) and Taeyong (NCT). Check out her astonishing moves on the M/V for *Uncover*.

EUNHYUK (SUPER JUNIOR)

Eunhyuk can breakdance, create charismatic performances with inspired moves, get super-dramatic with freestyle dance or show off some retro robot dance grooves. There is literally nothing that this Super Junior cannot do on the dance floor. He is the definition of having the moves.

HOSHI (SEVENTEEN)

Hoshi co-choreographs and teaches SEVENTEEN their dance moves, ensuring everyone is in time and on point. He is also the leader of their Performance Unit. We heart Hoshi!

Jimin in the BTS M/V for *Black Swan*.

JIMIN (BTS)

Jimin was the top of his dance class before he became a trainee. Jimin's effortless choreography showcases his contemporary dance and ballet skills. Check out his performances in *Lie*, *Serendipity* and *Black Swan* to see why Jimin was earning all the gold stars in class.

몬스타엑스

MONSTA X

Monsta X have marked their territory in K-Pop with a mash-up of hip-hop, R&B and pop sounds.

BACKGROUND

Monsta X are a six strong group, signed to Starship Entertainment. They were formed on a reality survival show called *No Mercy*. Their name can mean two things: 'Monsters' (who conquer K-Pop) and 'my star.'

They debuted in 2015 with their song *Trespass*, an aggressive mix of hip-hop, pop and R&B. There were originally seven members of Monsta X but in 2019 band member Wonho left the group. He was subsequently signed as a solo act with a subsidiary of Starship Entertainment, much to

his fans' relief!

Monsta X are known for curating a darker, more intense aura than your usual K-Pop group, they accentuate this with smokey eye make-up, eyeliner and fashion-forward outfit choices. These boys are not interested in the cutesy stereotypical image of K-Pop, their striking vocals, energetic confidence and big stage presence exudes big 'Monsta X' energy.

Monsta X give us monster vibes!

Wonho

Put your hands together for the Monsta X boys!

The iHeartRadio Jingle Ball performance made us heart Monsta X!

ACHIEVEMENTS

● Monsta X appeared in their first music show in 2017 for their song *Dramarama* and have gone on to win a number of awards such as MAMA Worldwide Icon of the Year in 2018.

● It should come as no surprise that Monsta X have a large number of international fans. They made their first US appearance at KCON LA and were the first K-Pop group to perform at the iHeartRadio Jingle Ball.

● They've also been nominated for a number of Western awards such as

Bringing the drama.

the MTV VMAs, MTV Europe Music Awards and Teen Choice Awards.

● The boys appeared on the Cartoon Network animated series *We Bare Bears*.

Teen Choice making the right choice.

FANS

● Monsta X's fans are called Monbebe, (French for My Baby). There are 4.3m of them on Twitter and 5.3m on Instagram and they are very passionate. Monbebes raised $20,000 to buy a billboard space in Times Square in an attempt to get Monsta X's label Starship Entertainment to keep Wonho in the group. Now that's loyalty bebe!

MONSTA X

JOOHONEY
주헌

Joohoney is one of the best rappers in K-Pop. He also acts and DJs. Despite his tough exterior he's a bit of a scaredy cat.
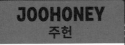 **We'll keep you safe, Joohoney!**

I.M
아이엠

I.M is the maknae of the group and is fluent in English, so he often speaks for the group when they have international promotions. He composes songs for Monsta X and released a mixtape *Be My Friend*, with Joohoney.
● **Be *OUR* friend, I.M!**

MINHYUK
민혁

Minhyuk writes and composes for the group. He is also a bit of a joker and pretends to be a weatherman.
● **Come rain or shine we're crazy about Minhyuk!**

HYUNGWON
형원

Before Monsta X, Hyungwon was a fashion model. Many memes have been made of his facial expressions. One of his side jobs is spinning decks as a DJ.
● **You have us in a spin, Hyungwon!**

SHOWNU
셔누

Shownu is the talented leader of the group, having been a JYP trainee for two years before moving to Starship. He's a super-gifted dancer.
● **We'll follow if Shownu is leader!**

KIHYUN
기현

Kihyun plays the piano, writes and produces tracks. He is an amazing cook and loves to tease his bandmates!
● **Kihyun is a super talent!**

FASHIONISTAS

K-Pop idols are dressed to kill in fashion to die for.

Korean idols are known for bringing high fashion and original choices into their looks. Idols often take traditional styles and pair them with street casual or more tailored pieces - think bubblegum hair with a twist of fusion hanbok. The result is fiercely original and always on point! The world has caught up with how fashion-forward K-Pop idols are: BLACKPINK are ambassadors for Celine, Dior and Chanel. BTS wore Dior on tour, and GQ mag declared Kai (EXO) as Best Dressed idol in 2020. Let's take a look at the K-pop idols having a fashion moment.

HWASA
(MAMAMOO)
is known for her controversial and daring fashion choices, and she always makes a big impact with her style.

HYUNA
The *Ice Cream* star's style is super trendy, stylish and fun.

KAI
(EXO)
Kai is known for combining luxury brands with simple cuts and being able to rock a crop top.

J-HOPE
(BTS)

J-Hope is known for wearing oversized street clothes, multi-coloured trainers and emo looks.

G-DRAGON
(BIG BANG)

G-Dragon loves to combine retail brands with high-end haute couture looks.

SUNMI

This solo star is not afraid to experiment with clashing patterns, colours and accessories. The bigger, the bolder, the better.

COOL COLLABS

K-Pop, collaborate and listen! Our East x West faves.

G-DRAGON & MISSY ELLIOTT

Hip-hop legend Missy Elliott featured on G-Dragon's track *Niliria* in 2013. The resulting sound brought together the high energy from two top MCs. They premiered the song at K-CON in LA, and the stage nearly combusted from such explosive vibes!

HWASA & DUA LIPA

When Dua Lipa appeared at the 2019 MAMA Awards, Hwasa performed her song *New Rules*. Dua clearly approved because Hwasa soon appeared on a remix of her hit song, *Physical*.

Hwasa at MAMA Awards.

Dua Lipa at MAMA Awards.

Halsey x BTS, BFF goals.

HALSEY

Halsey featured on the BTS track, *Boy With Luv*, in 2019. But the collaborations didn't stop there, Halsey then put the boys on her album, *Manic*, with a song called *Suga's Interlude*. Share the luv!

SNOOP DOGG

King of K-Pop, PSY collabed with rap icon Snoop Dogg on his track, *Hangover*. Snoop also featured on the remix of Girls' Generation's electropop track *The Boys* in 2011. K-Snoop!

PSY x Snoop Dogg all dressed up.

RM x Wale *Change.*

BTS & NICKI MINAJ

BTS's song *Idol* is already iconic for its fusion of traditional Korean sounds mixed with South African House - but did you know that Nicki Minaj is on the remix and appeared in the M/V?

RM & WALE

The leader of BTS, RM, and rapper Wale came together (after meeting on Twitter) to write the song *Change* in 2017. The song was ahead of its time where the rappers spoke about how they hoped for a better future.

LADY GAGA & BLACKPINK

Blackpink featured on Lady Gaga's song *Sour Candy*, from her 2020 album *Chromatica*. Our only disappointment is that there is no M/V. Now we're sour!

BTS & COLDPLAY

In 2021 BTS performed a cover of Coldplay's *Fix You* on MTV, prompting the bands to co-write *My Universe* together. It went straight to the top of the charts. Stratospheric!

블랙핑크

BLACKPINK

The girl group who won't settle for anything less than world domination!

BACKGROUND

BLACKPINK are arguably the biggest girl group in the world right now. They launched in 2016 under YG Entertainment and their debut album *Square One* featuring tracks *BOOMBAYAH* and *Whistle* were instant, catchy pop hits.

The name BLACKPINK comes from two meanings: 'pink' signifies their girly side and 'black' stands for strength and power. Their army of super fans are called 'BLINKS'.

In 2020 the girls released their eagerly anticipated first studio album called (original title alert!) *The Album*. Including hit songs *How You Like That*

and *Love Sick Girls* as well as features from Selena Gomez and Cardi B. It is always an event when BLACKPINK release an M/V since they are slick, high-budget, and look like the fashion pages of *Vogue* magazine!

To celebrate their album BLACKPINK released *Light Up The Sky*, a film documenting their journey from trainees to worldwide superstar musicians.

In 2021 the girls were acknowledged by the South Korean president as a global phenomenon. Impressive!

Taking a casual break from world domination.

Ddu-du Ddu-du we love BLACKPINK? Yes we Ddu.

ACHIEVEMENTS

● M/Vs for *Kill This Love* (2019) and *How You Like That* (2020) set viewing records within their first 24 hours.

● Their track *Sour Candy* with Lady Gaga debuted at number 33 on the Billboard Hot 100, the highest-charting debut song by a K-Pop girl group.

● BLACKPINK are currently the highest-charting female Korean act ever on the Billboard Hot 100, with

We want ice cream!

the release of *Ice Cream* feat. Selena Gomez. It peaked at number 13.

● They are the only K-Pop girl group to win the Song of the Summer VMA (for *How You Like That).*

● Their 2019 performance at Coachella was the first by a K-Pop girl group.

● They were named *Variety*'s Hitmaker Group of the Year.

● BLACKPINK became the first K-Pop girl group to have a million-selling album with *The Album*, with over 1.2m copies sold within a month of release.

How You Like That M/V.

BLACKPINK

ROSÉ
로제

Rosé auditioned in Australia before moving to Seoul to train as an idol for YG. She holds a world record for her M/V *On The Ground*.
● **We were on the ground after we heard that track!**

LISA
리사

LaLisa is the maknae of the group and is the most followed K-Pop idol on Insta with an incredible 43 million followers! She was part of the dance crew, We Zaa Cool.
● **No, you're Zaa Cool, Lisa!**

JENNIE
제니

Jennie is from New Zealand. She can play the flute, guitar and piano and is a fan of aerial yoga – a workout using suspended hammocks.
● **We'd love to hang out!**

JISOO
지수

Jisoo is the oldest member of the group. She plays the drums, acts, reads manga and likes playing computer games.
● **Jisoo is sooper cool.**

MONSTER ROOKIES

Breaking records, gaining widespread fandom and winning all the things – let's meet the best newbies.

M/V *Given-Taken*.

ENHYPEN

They were created from the show *I-land*, where fans from across the world voted on who would be in the final line-up of the latest group to join BigHit. Did you know that BTS and TXT were in the audience of the finale to see who would be their new labelmates?

Serving fierce looks.
Inset: Karina's avatar –
Æ Karina.

AESPA

This forward-thinking girl group from SM have everyone talking about them – why? Because they also have virtual counterparts. Fans will be able to interact with the avatars in online events, while the human members continue to promote their songs through concerts and signings.

ATEEZ were named '4th Generation Leaders' by the Korean government.

ATEEZ

You may know their songs *Hala Hala* and *Wonderland* but did you know that ATEEZ won an MTV EMA for Best Korean Act in 2019, just one year after their debut? Keep a close eye on what ATEEZ does next as we think these Idols are the next big thing in K-Pop.

ITZY

The latest girl group from JYP won on Mnet's *M!Countdown* just nine days after releasing their song *DALLA DALLA* and soon after achieved their first major music show win. All this less than two weeks after their debut puts them firmly in the record books.

TREASURE

This rookie group from YG Entertainment broke the record for most pre-orders, with 100,000 copies sold before anyone had even heard their debut song. When they debuted in August 2020 they already had 1.6m followers on Instagram!

Our treasures!

SuperM

슈퍼엠

Meet the star-studded super group making waves in the K-Pop world.

BACKGROUND

Dubbed a 'Super Boy Band,' SuperM are a group like no other. (Imagine a pick 'n' mix of the very best talent in the industry!).

SM Entertainment and Capitol Records brought together an incredible group of elite (the 'M' stands for master or matrix) idols borrowed from groups already at the top of their game.

The boys are truly international, with their debut taking place in L.A. and their first M/V filmed in Dubai.

Everyone wants a piece of SuperM,

M/V for 100.

even the WHO (who? the World Health Organisation), the group performed at their *Big Event* in 2020.

But don't worry, SHINee, EXO, NCT and WayV fans, the boys still perform in their original groups. Phew!

SuperM: seven super idols = seven times the star power.

Releasing their inner tigers: *Tiger Inside.*

ACHIEVEMENTS

● SuperM have only been active since 2019, but boy, have they been busy! Their debut EP *SuperM* smashed into the U.S. Billboard charts at No. 1 - the first Asian artists to do so with a debut (high-achievers much?).

● The band have already been on a world tour, and appeared on *The Ellen DeGeneres Show* twice.

Enter the matrix.

Ellen meeting the boys on her show.

● Their debut single *Jopping* was named one of Billboard's Best K-Pop Songs of the Year.

● In August 2020, SuperM won their first award - the Seoul Mayor Award at the 2020 Newsis K-Expo.

● SuperM are called the Avengers of K-Pop, as band members are strong on their own, but stronger together. They collabed with Marvel to release a limited edition collection, including clothes, bags and accessories.

SuperM

TEN
텐

Ten is Thai-Chinese and joined NCT in 2016 before joining WayV (NCT's Chinese sub-unit) in 2019. Aside from being an amazing singer and dancer, he's really good at art, is fluent in English and HATES fruit.
● **Ten doesn't eat his five a day!**

BAEKHYUN
변백현

Baekhyun is the leader of SuperM. He is one of the power vocals of EXO and has had even more success with his solo work *Candy*, *UN Village* and *Bambi*. Baekhyun has also acted, he is into martial arts, and has launched a clothes brand.
● **M-ulti-talented!**

LUCAS
루카스

Lucas is a rapper, singer and member of WayV and NCT U. He also released a solo track *Coffee Break*. Before he was an idol he used to be a model, which explains his position in SuperM as visual. Plus he speaks four languages!
● **We think Lucas is a model human!**

TAEMIN
이태민

Taemin was only 14 when he debuted in the legendary second-gen group SHINee in 2008. He has so many solo songs such as *MOVE*, *Criminal* and *WANT*. He is also best friends with Kai from EXO.
● **BFF legend!**

KAI
카이

Kai is from EXO and has some of the best dance talent in K-Pop. He released his solo album, *Kai*, in 2020. Kai is in a squad, a self-styled 'friendship parka' with Taemin, BTS's Jimin, and Ha Sungwoon They've been spotted hanging out at concerts and wearing matching coats.
● **Ultimate squad goals!**

MARK
마크

Mark auditioned in his native Canada and landed a spot rapping, singing, dancing and writing music for his group NCT U, before joining SuperM. He's collabed with Xiumin (EXO) and Parc Jae-jung.
● **Hands up, who's impressed?**

TAEYONG
이태용

Taeyong is a member of NCT. His roles are vocalist, rapper, visual and dancer! He released a solo song, *Long Flight*.
● **No excess baggage here!**

MOST LIT LIVE SHOWS EVER!

Daebak performances that K-fans will be talking about for years to come!

GD & TAEYANG *GOOD BOY* – MAMA 2014

This powerful performance of their hip-hop single, *Good Boy*, went viral when their lyrics made digs at the awards show where they were performing! Bold move boys!

CL & 2NE1 SURPRISE PERFORMANCE – MAMA 2015

CL opened the set solo with an explosive performance of her single *Hello B****es* before her band mates 2NE1 surprised the crowd by appearing on stage to slay with their long awaited comeback.

WANNA ONE – DEBUT STAGE 2017

This debut show at the Gocheok SkyDome was one of the biggest debut showcases in K-Pop history!

VIXX – MBC MUSIC FESTIVAL 2017

VIXX's Shangri-La remix at MBC Music Festival 2017 is undoubtedly one of the group's career highlights. Fans were impressed by the group wearing modernised hanbok (Korean traditional attire).

EXO *LOVE SHOT* – GAYO DAEJEON 2018

When EXO performed *Love Shot*, which started with a sizzling solo from Kai, they started trending in South Korea, and nearly broke YouTube.

BTS PERFORM FOR 37 MINUTES – 2019 MMA

On 30th November BTS turned the Melon Music Awards (MMA) into a BTS mini-concert. The phenomenal choreography took over a month to prepare and used 170 performers, 30 make-up artists and 218 costumes.

MULLET
MOMENTS

How do K-Pop idols make this hairstyle so hot?

JB (GOT7)
JB first rocked the mullet look in 2018 and returned it for GOT7's promotion of their studio album *Breath: Last Piece* in 2020. How does he manage to look cooler than all of us without even having to try?

Alfresco mullet.

Smooth mullet.

BAEKHYUN (EXO)
The EXO vocalist took fans by surprise when promoting *THE WAR* whilst sporting a mullet. The long red streaks give a feel-good vibe. Like it or love it, Baekhyun's mullet was serving the most stylish K-Pop vibes of summer 2017.

YEONJUN
(TXT) You have to have the face of an angel, and the confidence of Beyonce, to style a pink mullet with this cowboy hat.

Candyfloss mullet.

CHEN (EXO)

Another vocalist from EXO decided to give the mullet look a try during their video for *Tempo*. Chen chose a unique take, braiding the back portion of his hair adding a boho vibe. This look certainly got our attention!

Bowler mullet.

G-DRAGON (BIG BANG)

The King of K-Pop can pull off any look under the sun so is it even a surprise that he can pull off a mullet?

King mullet.

Messy mullet.

V (BTS)

Kim Taehyung would look good wearing a bin bag so naturally he can wear a mullet. Taehyung wore the controversial hairstyle in his video for *Singularity* as well the *Love Your: Tear* album promotions as a brunette and as a blond! Mullet-ty talented!

HYUNJIN (STRAY KIDS)

Some K-Pop fans like a "just rolled out bed" mullet. Lucky for them, that's the type of look that Hyunjin can easily pull off.

Fierce mullet.

THE8 (SEVENTEEN)

Mullets are popular! The8 revolutionised the hairstyle often only associated with washed-up rockers from the 80s! The8's cut transitioned easily from nerd to bad boy – who knew the mullet could be so versatile?

Casual mullet.

데이식스

DAY6

The K-Rock band giving us guitar riffs and energetic melodies blasting them into the rock star stratosphere.

BACKGROUND

Day6 are most definitely not your average K-Pop group. All five members write, compose and produce, and their sound is pure rock. We are talking guitar solos, heavy drum beats and lyrics to lift you up off your feet.

The band debuted in 2015 for JYP Entertainment, with EP *The Day*, and lead single *Congratulations*. A sixth member, keyboardist Junhyeok, left the group in February 2016.

In 2017 they launched a project,

Rocking out M/V Congratulations.

Every Day6, where they released two songs every month, promoted with concerts, music videos and broadcasts - even for K-Pop that's a lot of work! Rock on!

"Jae, you're looking the wrong way." Day6 trying to serve rock vibes.

M/V *Days Gone By.*

ACHIEVEMENTS

● Their debut EP, *The Day*, peaked at No.2 on Billboard's World Album Chart a week following its release and their first full-length album, *Sunrise*, was number 14 on Billboard's The 25 Greatest K-Pop Albums of the 2010s.

● The boys had their first music show win in July 2019. In the same year they also won Best Band Performance for *Time of Our Life* at the Genie Music Awards.

He's no Zombie!

● They have been nominated for best 'Rock Performance' at the Melon Music Awards every year since 2017.

● They also won the award for Best Idol Band at the Brand of The Year 2020.

● Day6 have also been nominated for awards at the Seoul Music Awards (2016), Golden Disc Awards (2019) and Asian Artist Awards (2020).

● Day6 won Best Band Performance for their song *Zombie* at the Mnet Asian Music Awards in 2020.

● Day6 have had two successful world tours (the *Youth* and *Gravity* tours).

● Day6's dedicated fans are MyDays, and will queue all day for a gig!

M/V *Time Of Our Life.*

DAY6

JAE
제이

Jae plays the guitar, sings and raps. He plays badminton and his nickname is 'Chicken Little' because, well, he looks like Chicken Little, what do you think? Jae has a YouTube channel and hosts the podcast *HOW DID I GET HERE*.

● **We don't know how you got here, Jae, but we're happy you did!**

SUNGJIN
성진

Sungjin is the leader, main vocal and plays the electric guitar. He loves playing sports, games and is a really good dancer. He has a Twitter account where he talks about the food he wants to eat!

● **Eat, play, sing, repeat ...**

DOWOON
도운

Dowoon plays the drums and is the maknae of the group. He studied at the Busan Arts College. When he's performing without a full drum kit, Dowoon plays a cajón, which is a drum that looks a bit like a box.

● **The beat goes on!**

YOUNG K
영케이

Young K plays bass, raps and is a vocalist. He moved to Toronto, Canada to attend high school and his original dream was to be a basketball player. He writes most of the music for Day6. He's also a radio DJ. Young K released his solo debut EP, *Eternal* in 2021.

● **He's talented, ok?**

WONPIL
원필

Wonpil plays the synthesizer, keyboards and is a vocalist. He used to be the maknae of the group, before Dowoon took the spot! He has a tattoo of a heart on his ring finger.

● **Wonpil has stolen our hearts!**

HANBOK FASHION

Showcasing Korean traditional pride K-Pop style.

K-Pop idols take style inspiration from everywhere and hanbok (the traditional clothing of South Korea) is no exception. Meet the idols giving a stylish nod to their proud Korean heritage.

We heart CLC's hanbok style.

CLC

The girls made their comeback in 2019 with fusion hanbok, mixing traditional coat and belt elements into K-Pop stage-worthy outfits.

VIXX

VIXX's 2017 comeback style was pure Korean fantasy, portrayed with modernised details and traditional hanbok materials. The choreography in their M/V saw the boys dancing with fans, and several hanbok looks.

Strong hanbok styling for VIXX.

BLACKPINK

In their first televised performance of *How You Like That*, BLACKPINK wore 2020's answer to the traditional hanbok, showcasing their look on Jimmy Fallon's *The Tonight Show*. Fire!

On *The Tonight Show: At Home Edition*.

BTS: Hands up for hanbok.

BTS

BTS showed serious hanbok style whilst promoting their track *Idol*. The outfits were so popular that they featured on BTS dolls!

A.C.E

A.C.E proudly displayed their heritage by wearing modern hanbok in the M/V for *Goblin: Favourite Boys*. They also incorporated Ssireum (Korean traditional wrestling) into their impressive choreography!

Our *Favourite Boys* in hanbok.

We are over the moon for hanbok!

OH MY GIRL

When they appeared on Mnet show *Queendom*, the group impressed the judges with their cover of Lovelyz's *Destiny* complete with scarf dancing and flowing hanbok fashions. Vibes!

TXT

TXT: *the group that captured the hearts (and ears) of a generation.*

BACKGROUND

TXT (Tomorrow By Together) formed in 2019 and were the second group to debut under BigHit Label. However, if you were expecting this quintet to be a carbon copy of BTS, you couldn't be more wrong. They have more of a bubbly, synth-pop sound which was perfectly exhibited by their debut single *Crown*. It broke the record for the most-liked K-Pop debut M/V in its first 24 hours, a record previously held by ITZY.

M/V for Crown.

They took home their first music show award within two weeks of their debut. The group have used their music to unpack the awkward, emotional pains of being a teenager.

TXT are called the It Boys of K-Pop. Whatever 'it' is, we want it!

Serving up some serious TXT vibes.

ACHIEVEMENTS

● TXT are the literal definition of Monster Rookies. In the year of their debut, they held a six-date showcase tour in the U.S., and took home more than 10 major music awards, including Rookie of the Year at the MMAs and Best New Male Artist at MAMA.

● They performed centre stage at Madison Square Garden at KCON – the world's largest fan celebration of Korean music and culture.

● TXT also released three albums that hit the top five of the Billboard World Album chart.

● Their debut album achieved the highest ever Billboard 200 Album chart ranking for a (male) K-Pop group.

● TXT are the first K-Pop group to ever be on the cover of Teen Vogue and have been interviewed at the Grammys. The TXT boys have been busy!

Blue Hour M/V.

FANS

● TXT's superfans are called MOA, which stands for 'Moments of Alwaysness', which we think is super cuteness!

● TXT already have an impressive 6.7m fans on Twitter AND 7.8m on Instagram. MOAs have been a loyal bunch to TXT from the very beginning.

● In 2019, when the group announced their first overseas tour, taking in six U.S. cities in two weeks, eager fans sold out the shows in under 24 hours!

TXT

SOOBIN
수빈

Soobin is the leader, rapper and dancer of TXT. He loves reading and has hosted several music shows. He's also a massive fan of Jin from BTS.
- **The host with the most!**

HUENING KAI
휴닝카이

Huening Kai is the maknae and visual of TXT. He was born in Hawaii, but grew up in China and S.Korea. His older sister Lea used to be a member of the K-Pop girl group VIVA.
- **Looks like being an idol runs in the family!**

YEONJUN
연준

Yeonjun is the oldest member of the group and he can rap, dance, sing, has great fashion sense and produces too! He also invented the TXT hand sign (you kind of make an 'X' with your fingers).
● **Super-talent Yeonjun.**

BEOMGYU
범규

Beomgyu may be young but he already has his own music production studio and is the person who normally brightens the mood in the group. He's a big BTS fan.
● **You brighten our day, Beomgyu!**

TAEHYUN
태현

Taehyun is considered to be the most mature, passionate and straight-talking member of TXT. He is incredibly smart and graduated with the highest grades in his year. As a child, Taehyun appeared in TV commercials.
● **He's got the smarts!**

FROM K-POP TO
K-DRAMA

Let's hope it's not just a stage they're going through!

Just like in Hollywood, there are many K-Pop idols that are good at bringing the (K-)drama. These idols are so talented they can't be contained to just one industry. Meet the triple threats crushing it in the TV world.

IU

Lee Ji-eun started acting in 2013 – five years after her singing debut – when she got the starring role in the rom-com series *You are the Best!* She also showed off her talent in the drama *My Mister* in 2018. IU has never heard of the phrase 'slay in your lane', she's slaying in all of them!

"Hello, *Hallyuwood is* calling."

HYUNGSIK

If you're a fan of K-dramas then you probably know (and love) this famous face. Park Hyung-sik is most famous for starring in the rom-com thriller series *Strong Woman Do Bong Soon*, the drama *Hwarang: The Poet Warrior Youth* and *Suits* (a Korean version of hit US show *Suits*). In fact, Hyungsik is so uber-amazing at acting that a lot of people forget he used to be in the group ZE:A! Now that's dramatic!

D.O. (EXO)

Do Kyungsoo (stage name D.O.) has been an Ultimate Bias of the Korean TV and film industry ever since he bagged 'Best New Actor' at the 3rd APAN Star Awards for his debut in the romance series *It's Okay, That's Love* in 2013. D.O. also showed off his mutli-talented acting chops with roles in comedy, muscials and period dramas. He's won so many awards he's run out of shelves! Leave some for the rest of the idols, D.O.!

Jinyoung forgot his lunchbox again!

JINYOUNG (GOT7)

Park Jinyoung burst onto the screen in coming-of-age show *Beloved Eun Dong*. His most recent role was in the hit fantasy thriller *He is Psychometric*, it was the first lead role that Jinyoung was cast in and the accolades came flooding in. Fun fact, Jinyoung was an actor before he was a member of GOT7. Seriously, is there anything he can't do?

Let's all join the Hwarang gang!

V (BTS)

Kim Taehyung made his acting debut in 2016 with the internationally popular coming of age drama *Hwarang: the Poet Warrior Youth* along with Park Seo Joon, Park Hyung-sik and Choi Minho (from SHINee). That was one gorgeous cast!

YOONA (GIRLS' GENERATION)

Im Yoon-ah has taken on roles in both TV and film and yes, you guessed it, crushed it every time. She's taken home awards for Best New Actress and has starred in some of South Korea's highest grossing films (the ones that make the most money, not actually gross ...).

The award goes to ...

IDOLS
ON OUR WATCH

The groups on the rise to the top of the K-Pop lists.

K-Pop is a frenetic, fast-paced, bubblegum music scene, with new music and bands popping into existence all the time. It's hard to keep track of them all, but we've got you! Sit back and read about your next Bias, and you'll be a bona fide superfan!

EVERGLOW

If you haven't heard of Everglow yet then we strongly suggest you listen to their song *Bon Bon Chocolat* immediately, like NOW! An energetic electronic and hip-hop influenced track with a killer drop and strong vocals from the girls. The M/V has over 53m YouTube views. That's a lot of fans, are you ready for your Everglow up?

Oh Really? OK!

N.Flying

If you like rock music, then you need to pay attention to N.Flying's awesome M/Vs. Check out their songs *Autumn Dream* and *Oh Really*.

KARD

A co-ed group is rare in K-Pop, but it only adds to KARD's appeal. They debuted with EP *Hola Hola* to critial acclaim. Pre-debut single *Oh Na Na* will have you rocking out in your living room. Oh yes, yes!!!

CRAVITY

Cravity only debuted in 2020, but they came out of the gates swinging. Named Brightest Potential at the 2020 Asia Music Awards and taking 12th place on the Billboard Top Social 50 list. They're ones to watch.

M/V *My Turn.*

A.C.E

Go watch M/V *Goblin: Favourite Boys* to understand why A.C.E have been declared one of the K-Pop groups to watch by *Teen Vogue* and *Rolling Stone India*. Their recent album drop *Changer: Dear Eris* has perfect catchy beats for the summer sands of Ibiza.

LOONA

Loona are arguably the hottest new girl group with the best dancers in K-Pop. You need to check out their dance covers of NCT 127's *Cherry Bomb* and BTS's *Not Today*. Is there a routine they can't do? Surely not?!

BLACKSWAN

The group (known as Rania at the time) was put together by American musician and producer Teddy Riley in 2011. They underwent a rebrand in June 2020 and emerged as Blackswan. DR Music took an unusual turn and debuted member Fatou, who is from Senegal. She is the only Black K-Pop star currently in the industry and the second to ever appear in K-Pop. We hope to see more black idols in the future of K-Pop music.

M/V *Tonight.*

K-POP
ESSENTIAL STREAMS

Consider this your K-Pop starter pack!

1

SHINee, *1 of 1*
Released in 2016, SHINee was definitely inspired by the music of the 1990s.

2

Girls' Generation, *Gee*
The perfect electro pop dance bop! Get your dancing shoes on.

3

Big Bang, *BANG BANG BANG*
Stand on a table and sing along with this one.

4

CL, *5 Star*
CL displays a more romantic side in this love-filled pop groove.

5

BTS, *HOME*
BTS express the need for peace of mind and wanting to be with their loved ones.

6

EXO, *The Eve*
An effortlessly cool song that will have you doing body rolls in your bedroom.

7

GOT7, *You Calling My Name*
The definition of a smooth R&B track with a hard bassline. Sway sway!

8

ITZY, *Not Shy*
A girl power anthem about being who you are and doing what you want! Yass!

9

Wonho, *Open Mind*
A dangerous lyrical invitation over a groovy, funk-fuelled beat.

10

TWICE, *More & More*
A Latin-inspired house track about the honeymoon phase of a relationship.

11

Kai, *Mmmh*
R&B track all about how you can instantly like someone you just met.

12

TXT, *We Lost The Summer*
TXT are reflecting on staying at home over a dance-hall inspired beat.

13

Pentagon, *Runaway*
Power-boosting song inspiring people to know they'll be OK.

14

Mamamoo, *Dingga*
A retro-inspired song about wanting to enjoy life and being with friends!

15

iKon, *Love Scenario*
You'd never think that iKon were talking about a break-up in this track.

16

**Eric Nam,
*I Don't Miss You***
The break-up anthem we all needed in our lives.

17

IU feat Suga (BTS), *Eight*
Singing about the uncertainty of turning 28, the age both artists are.

18

NCT 127, *Kick It*
This hip-hop dance track makes you want to do kung-fu like Bruce Lee!

19

**Super Junior feat.
Leslie Grace, *Lo Siento***
Changing the game with this Latin K-Pop track.

20

Irene & Seulgi, *Monster*
Addictive yet haunting track that sounds like a song from a scary movie.

21

Weeekly, *After School*
Listen to this upbeat track and you can't help but feel uplifted and happy.

CREDITS

Front Cover: PICTURES: Imaginechina Limited / Alamy Images, Newscom / Alamy Images, WENN Rights Ltd / Alamy Images, Everett Collection Inc. / Alamy Images, REUTERS / Alamy Images, Erik Pendzich / Alamy Images.

Back Cover: PICTURES: Imaginechina Limited / Alamy Images, Newscom / Alamy Images, MediaPunch Inc. / Alamy Images.

4-5: PICTURES: Everett Collection Inc. / Alamy Images, Top Photo Corporation / Alamy Images, Newscom / Alamy Images, Imaginechina Limited / Alamy Images.

6-7: WORDS: Ontheaside.com: Jeremy Mersereau, Teenvogue.com: Crystal Bell, Nchschant.com: Angela Canales.
PICTURES: Monument, Bando Records.

8-9: WORDS: Wikipedia.org, Bandwagon.asia: Christy Chua, Eonline.com: Charmaine Tan, Thekrazemagazine.com: Annika Brandes.
PICTURES: Aflo Co. Ltd. / Alamy Images, REUTERS / Alamy Images, PA Images / Alamy Images, REUTERS / Alamy Images, Top Photo Corporation / Alamy Images, The Photo Access / Alamy Images.

10-11: PICTURES: Top Photo Corporation / Alamy Images, Newscom / Alamy Images, Imaginechina Limited / Alamy Images, Newscom / Alamy Images, Big Hit Music.

12-15: WORDS: Rollingstoneindia.com: Riddhi Chakraborty.
PICTURES: Image Press Agency / Alamy Images, ZUMA Press, Inc. / Alamy Images, REUTERS / Alamy Images, Big Hit Music.

16-17: PICTURES: Newscom / Alamy Images, Top Photo Corporation / Alamy Images, WENN Rights Ltd / Alamy Images, Million Market Inc., MediaPunch Inc. / Alamy Images, Newscom / Alamy Images, Beginner Records.

18-19: WORDS: Koreaboo.com, Hankyung.com, Wikipedia.org.
PICTURES: SM Entertainment., Ltd., YG Entertainment Inc., Big Hit Music, ZUMA Press, Inc. / Alamy Images

20-23: WORDS: Soompi.com: J. K (ilmare42), Soompi.com: C. Hong.
PICTURES: REUTERS / Alamy Images, Newscom / Alamy Images, Newscom / Alamy Images, Sipa US / Alamy Images.

24-25: WORDS: Soompi.com: M. Dang, Kpopstarz.com: Staff reporter.
PICTURES: Imaginechina Limited / Alamy Images, Top Photo Corporation / Alamy Images, Newscom / Alamy Images, SM Entertainment., Ltd., YG Entertainment, Big Hit Music.

26-29: WORDS: Gq-magazine.co.uk: Taylor Glasby, Kprofiles.com, Wikipedia.org.
PICTURES: ZUMA Press, Inc. / Alamy Images, Sipa US / Alamy Images, The Photo Access / Alamy Images, Image Press Agency / Alamy Images, Aflo Co. Ltd. / Alamy Images, Starship Entertainment.

30-31: WORDS: Gq-magazine.co.uk: Zak Maoui, Soompi.com: Caromalis, Koreaboo.com: Mikayla Berry.
PICTURES: WENN Rights Ltd / Alamy Images, Newscom / Alamy Images, Aflo Co. Ltd. / Alamy Images, dpa picture alliance / Alamy Images.

32-33: WORDS: Sbs.com.au, Dazeddigital.com: Christine Jun.
PICTURES: ZUMA Press, Inc. / Alamy Images, MNET Media Corp. & YG Entertainment Inc., RBW Inc., WMG, Big Hit Music, YG Entertainment Inc.

34-37: WORDS: Wikipedia.org.
PICTURES: Everett Collection Inc. / Alamy Images, Imaginechina Limited / Alamy Images, YG Entertainment Inc.

38-39: WORDS: Teenvogue.com: Natasha Mulenga, Pinkvilla.com: Ishani Sarkar, Wikipedia.org.
PICTURES: ZUMA Press, Inc. / Alamy Images, Newscom / Alamy Images, HYBE Co., Ltd, SM Entertainment., Ltd., YG Entertainment Inc.

40-43: WORDS: Wikipedia.org, Kprofiles.com/super-m-profile-facts.
PICTURES: REUTERS / Alamy Images, Newscom / Alamy Images, SM Entertainment., Ltd., UMG, The Ellen Show.

44-45: WORDS: Soompi.com: S. Park, Allkpop.com: Mssylee, Kbizoom.com.
PICTURES: MNET Media Corp. & YG Entertainment Inc., Genie Music, Jellyfish Entertainment, SM Entertainment., Ltd., Big Hit Music.

46-47: WORDS: Soompi.com: Hgordon, Koreaboo.com: Alicia Valley.
PICTURES: Imaginechina Limited / Alamy Images, JYP Entertainment Inc., SM Entertainment., Ltd., HYBE Co., Ltd., Big Hit Music.

48-51: WORDS: Mtv.com/news: Crystal Bell, Kprofiles.com, Wikipedia.org.
PICTURES: Top Photo Corporation / Alamy Images, REUTERS / Alamy Images, CUBE Entertainment, Jellyfish Entertainment, YG Entertainment Inc., The Tonight Show, JYP Entertainment Inc.

52-53: WORDS: Koreaboo.com: Jasmine Turner, Vogue.co.uk: Natasha Mulenga.
PICTURES: Newscom / Alamy Images, Big Hit Music, The Tonight Show, SM Entertainment., Ltd., MNET Media Corp., WOOLLIM Entertainment, WM Entertainment.

54-57: WORDS: Koreaboo.com, Teenvogue.com: Sara Delgado, Wikipedia.org, Kprofiles.com.
PICTURES: Newscom / Alamy Images, REUTERS / Alamy Images, Big Hit Music.

58-59: WORDS: Bandwagon.asia: Christy Chua, Soompi.com: Binahearts.
PICTURES: Newscom / Alamy Images, Aflo Co. Ltd. / Alamy Images, tvN, KBS, JTBC.

60-61: WORDS: Hellokpop.com: Kirsten, Thehoneypop.com: Carly Ho, Wikipedia.org.
PICTURES: Newscom / Alamy Images, ZUMA Press, Inc. / Alamy Images, Top Photo Corporation / Alamy Images, Danal Entertainment Inc., Kakao Entertainment.

62-63: PICTURES: SM Entertainment., Ltd., Big Hit Music, YG Entertainment Inc., JYP Entertainment Inc., Highline Entertainment, Kakao M, Big Hit Music/Hybe, Cube Entertainment, Rainbow Bridge World, Genie Music, Universal Music Group, The Orchard Music.